W9-ACD-360

CABARET

RANDOM HOUSE · NEW YORK

Harold Prince's

CABARET

───────── ☆ ─────────

Book by Joe Masteroff

Music by John Kander

Lyrics by Fred Ebb

Based on the play by John van Druten

and stories by Christopher Isherwood

CABARET was first presented on November 20, 1966, by Harold Prince in association with Ruth Mitchell at the Broadhurst Theatre in New York City, with the following cast:

(In order of appearance)

MASTER OF CEREMONIES (EMCEE)	Joel Grey
CLIFFORD BRADSHAW	Bert Convy
ERNST LUDWIG	Edward Winter
CUSTOMS OFFICER	Howard Kahl
FRAULEIN SCHNEIDER	Lotte Lenya
FRAULEIN KOST	Peg Murray
HERR SCHULTZ	Jack Gilford
GIRL	Tresha Kelly
SALLY BOWLES	Jill Haworth
GIRL ORCHESTRA	Maryann Burns, Janice Mink, Nancy Powers, Viola Smith, Mary Ehara, Rita O'Connor
TWO LADIES	
MAITRE D'	Frank Bouley
MAX	John Herbert
BARTENDER	Ray Baron
GERMAN SAILORS	Bruce Becker, Steven Boockvor, Roger Briant, Edward Nolfi
FRAU WENDEL	Mara Landi
HERR WENDEL	Eugene Morgan
FRAU KRUGER	Miriam Lehmann-Haupt
HERR ERDMANN	Sol Frieder
KIT KAT GIRLS:	
MARIA	Pat Gosling
LULU	Lynn Winn
ROSIE	Bonnie Walker
FRITZIE	Marianne Selbert

TEXAS	Kathie Dalton
FRENCHIE	Barbara Alston
BOBBY	Jere Admire
VICTOR	Bert Michaels
GRETA	Jayme Mylroie
FELIX	Robert Sharp

Directed by Harold Prince

Dances and cabaret numbers by Ronald Field

Scenery by Boris Aronson

Costumes by Patricia Zipprodt

Lighting by Jean Rosenthal

Musical direction by Harold Hastings

Orchestrations by Don Walker

Dance arrangements by David Baker

SCENE: Berlin, Germany

TIME: 1929–1930. Before the start of the Third Reich

NOTE: There is no curtain. As the audience enters the theatre, the stage is bare and dark. Street lamps on both sides of the stage recede dimly into the distance. A large mirror hanging center stage reflects the auditorium, thus allowing the audience to see itself. A spiral staircase is on the left side of the proscenium arch.

Musical Numbers

Act One

"Willkommen"	EMCEE and the Company
"So What?"	FRAULEIN SCHNEIDER
"Don't Tell Mama"	SALLY and the GIRLS
"Telephone Song"	The Company
"Perfectly Marvelous"	SALLY and CLIFF
"Two Ladies"	EMCEE and TWO LADIES
"It Couldn't Please Me More"	FRAULEIN SCHNEIDER and HERR SCHULTZ
"Tomorrow Belongs to Me"	EMCEE and WAITERS
"Why Should I Wake Up?"	CLIFF
"The Money Song"	EMCEE and the Cabaret GIRLS
"Married"	FRAULEIN SCHNEIDER and HERR SCHULTZ
"Meeskite"	HERR SCHULTZ
"Tomorrow Belongs to Me" (Reprise)	FRAULEIN KOST, ERNST and GUESTS

Act Two

"If You Could See Her"	EMCEE and the GIRLS
"Married" (Reprise)	HERR SCHULTZ
"If You Could See Her" (Reprise)	EMCEE and BOBBY
"What Would You Do?"	FRAULEIN SCHNEIDER
"Cabaret"	SALLY
Finale	CLIFF, SALLY, FRAULEIN SCHNEIDER, HERR SCHULTZ, EMCEE and the Company

Act One

SCENE I

*In the darkness, a large sign is illuminated—letter by letter.
It reads: Cabaret. Then it disappears.*

There is a roll of the drums. Then the MASTER OF CERE-
MONIES (EMCEE) *enters in a spotlight up stage. He is a bizarre
little figure—much lipstick, much rouge, patent-leather hair
parted in the middle. He walks toward the footlights and greets
the audience.*

EMCEE (*Singing*)
    Willkommen, bienvenue, welcome
    Fremde, étranger, stranger
    Glücklich zu sehen
    Je suis enchanté
    Happy to see you
    Bleibe, reste, stay
    Willkommen, bienvenue, welcome
    Im Cabaret, au Cabaret, to Cabaret!

Meine Damen und Herren—Mesdames et Messieurs
—Ladies and Gentlemen! Guten abend—bon soir—good
evening! Wie geht's? Comment ça va? Do you feel good?
Ich bin euer confrencier—je suis votre compère—I am your
host! (*He sings again*)
    Und sage—
    Willkommen, bienvenue, welcome
    Im Cabaret, au Cabaret, to Cabaret!

Leave your troubles outside! So—life is disappointing? Forget it! In here life is beautiful—the girls are beautiful—

3

even the orchestra is beautiful! (A GIRL ORCHESTRA *appears on stage and plays a chorus of "Willkommen"*) And now —presenting the Cabaret Girls! (*The* GIRLS *enter. The mirror tilts upward—reflecting the stage rather than the auditorium*) Each and every one a virgin. You don't believe me? Well, don't take my word for it. Go ahead. Ask her! Outside it is winter. But here it is so hot—every night we have the battle to keep the girls from taking off all their clothing. So don't go away. Who knows? Tonight we may lose the battle!

GIRLS (*Singing*)
    Wir sagen—
    Willkommen, bienvenue, welcome
    Im Cabaret, au Cabaret, to Cabaret!

EMCEE
    And now to serve you—
        (WAITERS, BUSBOYS, ENTERTAINERS *appear*)

ALL (*Singing*)
    Willkommen, bienvenue, welcome
    Fremde, étranger, stranger
    Glücklich zu sehen
    Je suis enchanté
    Happy to see you
    Bleibe, reste, stay
    Willkommen, bienvenue, welcome
    Im Cabaret, au Cabaret, to Cabaret!

    Blackout

A compartment of a European railway train. It appears to be in motion.

CLIFFORD BRADSHAW *is alone in the compartment—asleep. He is in his late twenties, pleasant-looking, intelligent, reserved. His suitcase and portable typewriter are on the rack above his head.*

ERNST LUDWIG *enters. He is German, about thirty, friendly and likable. He carries a suitcase, a brown leather briefcase and a magazine. He seems rather nervous.*

ERNST Occupied?   (CLIFF *opens his eyes and shakes his head*) It is permitted?

CLIFF   Please.
(ERNST *places his suitcase on the rack over the seat opposite* CLIFF. *He puts his briefcase on the floor beside his legs as he sits down*)

ERNST   English?

CLIFF   American.

ERNST   German. Berlin. Ernst Ludwig.
(*They shake hands*)

CLIFF   Clifford Bradshaw. Pennsylvania. Are we slowing down for the German border?

ERNST Ja.

CLIFF You've taken this trip before?

ERNST Many many times. (ERNST *shows increasing signs of nervousness*) You are a tourist?

CLIFF *No!* Not exactly. I'm a writer and I give English lessons. (*The train stops.* ERNST *gets up and surveys the corridor*) Would you care for a cigarette? (*There is no answer*) Herr Ludwig?

ERNST (*Absently*) Ja?

CLIFF A cigarette?

ERNST No. Thank you.
(ERNST *suddenly sits down and pretends to be absorbed in a magazine. Two German* CUSTOMS OFFICERS *enter the compartment*)

OFFICER Deutsche Grenzkontrolle. Ihre pässe bitte.

CLIFF I beg your pardon?

OFFICER Your passport, if you please. (CLIFF *hands his passport to the* OFFICER) Welcome to Germany, Mr. Bradshaw. (*The* OFFICER *indicates* CLIFF's *bags*) Yours? (CLIFF *nods. The* OFFICER *puts a Customs mark on his bags without even taking them off the rack. Then he turns to* ERNST, *who is*

6

deep in his magazine) Ihren pass, bitte. (ERNST *hands over his passport)* Sie waren geschäftlich in Paris?

ERNST   Nein. Auf einer urlaubreise.

OFFICER   Offen sie ihre tasche. (ERNST *takes down his suitcase and opens it. The* OFFICER *goes through it. While the* OFFICER's *back is turned* ERNST *takes his briefcase off the floor and puts it on the rack over* CLIFF's *head.* CLIFF *is surprised, but says nothing. The* OFFICER *marks* ERNST's *bag)* Haben sie nur diese eine tasche?

ERNST   Ja. Das ist alles.

OFFICER   *(To* CLIFF*)*   I wish you will enjoy your stay in Germany. And a most Happy New Year. *(The* OFFICER *exits.* ERNST, *very relieved, retrieves the briefcase)*

CLIFF   What's in the bag?

ERNST   *(Too casual)*   What? Baubles from Paris: perfume . . . silk stockings . . . But more than is permitted. You understand?

CLIFF   *(Nods)*   I guess I've done a little smuggling myself.

ERNST   *(With new vigor)*   You are most understanding. I thank you very much. And I would like to see to it that Berlin will open its arms to you! We begin tonight—New

Year's Eve—the Kit Kat Klub! The hottest spot in Berlin. Telephones on every table. Girls call you. You call them. Instant connections.

CLIFF (*Shaking his head*) Thanks—but I've still got to find a room.

ERNST You have no room! But this is no problem! (*He takes out a card and writes on it*) I know the finest residence in all Berlin. Just tell Fraulein Schneider that Ernst Ludwig has recommended you.

CLIFF I can't afford the finest residence in Berlin. I need something inexpensive.

ERNST But this *is* inexpensive! Very inexpensive! She has this kind of room and that kind of room. Absolute satisfaction!

CLIFF I don't care if it's awful—as long as it's cheap.

ERNST But this *is* awful. You will love it!
(*The train starts again.* ERNST *hands* CLIFF *the card.* CLIFF *reads it*)

CLIFF Fraulein Schneider . . .

ERNST You see! You see! You have a new friend—Ernst Ludwig! You have a fine place to live! And you have perhaps even your first English pupil! (*He indicates himself.* CLIFF *is quite surprised*) Ja! So welcome to Berlin, my friend. Welcome to Berlin! (*They shake hands. The train moves upstage and disappears as the* EMCEE *crosses downstage*)

EMCEE (*Singing*)
  Welcome to Berlin!
  Willkommen, bienvenue, welcome
  Fremde, étranger, stranger
  Glücklich zu sehen
  Je suis enchanté
  Happy to see you
  Bleibe, reste, stay!

A room in FRAULEIN SCHNEIDER's *flat. The furnishings are ugly and ponderous: a bed, a table with two chairs, an armoire, and, behind a curtain, a washstand.*

As the lights come up, FRAULEIN SCHNEIDER *enters. She is about sixty: full of vitality, interested in everything, probably indestructible. She wears a flowered dressing gown and carpet slippers.*

CLIFF *follows her, carrying his bags.*

FRAULEIN SCHNEIDER   You see! All comforts! And with break-fast only one hundred marks!

CLIFF   It's very nice, Fraulein Schneider. In fact—too nice. You don't have something cheaper?

FRAULEIN SCHNEIDER   But for a friend of Herr Ludwig . . .

CLIFF   I've very little money.

FRAULEIN SCHNEIDER   But you will give English lessons. Many pupils will come. And they will pay you. And then you will pay *me*. No?

CLIFF (*Shaking his head*)   Fifty marks. That's my absolute limit. (FRAULEIN SCHNEIDER *shrugs her shoulders*) If you've

anything else . . . I don't care how small, how far from the
bathroom . . .

FRAULEIN SCHNEIDER   But for a *professor*—this is more suitable.

CLIFF   I am *not* a professor. Think of me as a starving author.
What do you have for a starving author?

FRAULEIN SCHNEIDER   An author! A poet! You have the look!

CLIFF   A novelist.

FRAULEIN SCHNEIDER   And you will be most famous. There is
no doubt. You will have *this* room. Here is for your clothing.
Look—there is even a table for writing. Come . . . sitz.
(*She pulls out the chair at the writing table and invites*
CLIFF *to try it. He does*) Good? (CLIFF *nods*) You need a
cushion . . . (*She stuffs a cushion in behind him*) Besser?
(*Then she stands back and admires the scene*) A novelist!
It is like—years ago—when in all my rooms—persons of real
quality . . .

CLIFF   But I can still only pay fifty marks.

FRAULEIN SCHNEIDER   This room is worth one hundred.
More than one hundred. (*She looks at* CLIFF *hopefully.*
He shakes his head) Fifty? (CLIFF *nods*. FRAULEIN
SCHNEIDER *suddenly surrenders*) Sitz! (*She sings*)

You say fifty marks,
I say one hundred marks;
A difference of fifty marks,

Why should that stand in our way?
As long as the room's to let,
The fifty that I will get
Is fifty more than I had yesterday, ja?
When you're as old as I—
Is anyone as old as I?
What difference does it make?
An offer comes, you take.

For the sun will rise and the moon will set,
And you learn how to settle for what you get.
It'll all go on if we're here or not,
So who cares? So what?
So who cares? So what?

When I was a girl my summers were spent by the sea,
     so what?
And I had a maid doing all of the housework, not me,
     so what?
Now I scrub up the floors and I wash down the walls,
And I empty the chamber pot.
If it ended that way then it ended that way, and I shrug
     and I say, so what?

For the sun will rise and the moon will set,
And you learn how to settle for what you get.
It'll all go on if we're here or not,
So who cares, so what?
So who cares, so what?

When I had a man, my figure was boyish and flat,
     so what?
Through all of our years he was so disappointed in that,
     so what?

Now I have what he missed and my bosom is full,
But he lies in a churchyard plot.
If it wasn't to be that he ever would see the
    abundance of me,
So what?

For the sun will rise and the moon will set,
And you learn how to settle for what you get.
It'll all go on if we're here or not,
So who cares, so what?
So who cares, so what?

So once I was rich, and now all my fortune is gone,
    so what?
And love disappeared and only the memory lives on,
    so what?
If I've lived through all that, and I've lived through
    all that,
Fifty marks doesn't mean a lot.
If I like that you're here, and I like that you're here,
Happy New Year, my dear, so what?

For the sun will rise and the moon will set,
And you learn how to settle for what you get.
It'll all go on if we're here or not,
So who cares . . . so what?
So who cares . . . so what?
It all goes on,
So who cares? Who cares? Who cares? So what?

(FRAULEIN SCHNEIDER *starts checking the room. She takes
out a blanket*) An additional blanket. The telephone is in the
hall. I will bring towels. (*There is a knock on the door*)
Come in!

(FRAULEIN KOST *enters. She is thirtyish, a large and happy woman who works diligently at her profession*)

FRAULEIN KOST Fraulein Schneider! There you are! There is no hot water in the bathroom! The second time this week!

FRAULEIN SCHNEIDER (*To* CLIFF) If you will excuse me, Herr Bradshaw.

FRAULEIN KOST (*She notes* CLIFF *and starts giving him the eye*) So you have finally rented this room.

FRAULEIN SCHNEIDER Here is Herr Clifford Bradshaw—the world-famous American novelist.
(FRAULEIN KOST *starts toward* CLIFF. FRAULEIN SCHNEIDER *steps between them*)

CLIFF How do you do?

FRAULEIN KOST (*Flirtatiously*) I am Fraulein Kost. Across the hall . . . Please feel free at any time . . . (*A* GERMAN SAILOR *runs in*)

SAILOR (*To Fraulein Kost*) Schatzi—where are you . . . ?
(FRAULEIN KOST *is a little embarrassed to have* CLIFF *see the* SAILOR)

FRAULEIN KOST (*Making it up quickly*) My nephew! He is visiting me. From Hamburg.

FRAULEIN SCHNEIDER (*To* FRAULEIN KOST) Come! We talk outside. We are disturbing Herr Bradshaw. And bring your nephew with you—from Hamburg! (*When they are gone, she turns back to* CLIFF) My apologies, Herr Bradshaw. I guarantee she will not bother you again.

CLIFF Bother me?
(*There is a knock at the door*)

FRAULEIN SCHNEIDER What is it now?
(HERR SCHULTZ *enters. He is in his fifties, very warm and cheerful. He dresses neatly, but it would appear that he needs a woman to tell him what tie goes with what. He is carrying a bottle of schnapps*)

SCHULTZ Fraulein Schneider—

FRAULEIN SCHNEIDER Ah, Herr Schultz! Is it eleven o'clock? I have been showing Herr Bradshaw his room. Herr Bradshaw—Herr Schultz, who also lives here.

CLIFF Pleased to meet you.

SCHULTZ Honored!

FRAULEIN SCHNEIDER Herr Bradshaw is from America.

SCHULTZ America! I have a cousin in Buffalo.

FRAULEIN SCHNEIDER And Herr Schultz is proprietor of the finest fruit market on the Nollendorfplatz.

SCHULTZ Seville oranges. Delicious.

FRAULEIN SCHNEIDER I will dress now. (*To* CLIFF) Herr Schultz has been kind enough to invite me to join him in a glass of schnapps for the New Year.

SCHULTZ And a little fruit.

FRAULEIN SCHNEIDER And—after all—why not? Otherwise I am in bed with a hot-water bottle.

SCHULTZ Perhaps Herr Bradshaw . . .

CLIFF No. But thanks for asking.

SCHULTZ Another time! (SCHULTZ *shakes hands with* CLIFF) I want to wish you *mazel* in the New Year.

CLIFF *Mazel?*

SCHULTZ Jewish. It means luck!

CLIFF Thank you. The same to you.

SCHULTZ I come to you, Fraulein—in ten minutes—with the schnapps!

FRAULEIN SCHNEIDER And the fruit! (HERR SCHULTZ *exits.* FRAULEIN SCHNEIDER *turns to* CLIFF) And now—please— anything you require—knock on my door. Day, night. Also —welcome to Berlin!
  (*She exits*)

CLIFF Welcome to Berlin—famous novelist. (*He puts his typewriter on the table*) Open the Remington . . .
(*A beautiful* GIRL *appears, sitting at a café table. She is singing into a telephone. She does not look at* CLIFF)

GIRL Hello? Hello?
(CLIFF *is unaware of the* GIRL. *He looks gloomily at the typewriter*)

CLIFF That's what you came here for.

GIRL (*singing*)
Sitting all alone like that,
You happened to catch my eye.
Would you like to buy a girl a drink?
(CLIFF *opens the typewriter half-heartedly*)

CLIFF Welcome to Berlin—famous novelist . . .

GIRL (*singing*)
Ja? You would? Come on over!
(CLIFF *closes the typewriter, takes his coat, and exits out the door*)

SCENE 4

The GIRL *is sitting in the middle of the Kit Kat Klub, an establishment in which all the tables have telephones on them so that guests can call each other. At the moment, the Klub is packed. It is New Year's Eve, 1930.*

CLIFF *enters the Klub and is seated at a table. The* EMCEE *appears; there is a fanfare from the* GIRL ORCHESTRA.

EMCEE   Meine Damen und Herren—Mesdames et Messieurs —Ladies and Gentlemen— And now the Kit Kat Klub is proud to present a beautiful young lady from England. She is so beautiful, so talented, so charming that I have asked her to marry me. And now there is only one thing standing in our way: my wife! (*He pantomimes cutting his throat. A few members of the audience laugh*) I give you: the toast of Mayfair—Fraulein Sally Bowles!

(SALLY BOWLES *enters. She is in her early twenties, rather pretty, rather sophisticated, rather child-like, exasperating and irresistible*)

SALLY (*Singing*)
   Mama thinks I'm living in a convent,
   A secluded little convent
   In the southern part of France.
   Mama doesn't even have an inkling
   That I'm working in a nightclub
   In a pair of lacey pants.

18

So please, sir, if you run into my mama,
Don't reveal my indiscretion—
Give a working girl a chance.
Hush up, don't tell Mama,
Shush up, don't tell Mama,
Don't tell Mama whatever you do.

If you had a secret,
You bet I could keep it.
I would never tell on you.
I'm breaking every promise that I gave her,
So won't you kindly do a girl a great big favor?

And please, my sweet patater,
Keep this from the mater,
Though my dance is not against the law.

You can tell my papa, that's all right,
'Cause he comes in here every night,
But don't tell Mama what you saw!
  (*The* CABARET GIRLS *appear*)

GIRLS (*Singing*)
  Mama thinks I'm on a tour of Europe
  With a couple of my school-chums
  And a lady chaperone.
  Mama doesn't even have an inkling
  That I left them all in Antwerp
  And I'm touring on my own.
  So please, sir, if you run into my mama,

Don't reveal my indiscretion—
Just leave well enough alone.

GIRLS

Hush up—

SALLY

Don't tell Mama.

GIRLS

Shush up—

SALLY

Don't tell Mama

SALLY and **GIRLS**

Don't tell Mama whatever you do.

SALLY

If you had a secret,
You bet I could keep it.

GIRLS

We would never tell on you.

SALLY

You wouldn't want to get me in a pickle,
And have her go and cut me off without a nickel,

SALLY and **GIRLS**

So let's trust one another.

Keep this from my mother,
Though I'm still as pure as mountain snow.

SALLY

You can tell my uncle, here and now,
'Cause he's my agent anyhow.

GIRLS

But don't tell Mama what you know.

SALLY

You can tell my grandma, suits me fine,
Just yesterday she joined the line.

GIRLS

But don't tell Mama what you know.

SALLY

You can tell my brother, that ain't grim,
'Cause if he squeals on me, I'll squeal on him.

SALLY and GIRLS

But don't tell Mama, bitte,
Don't tell Mama, please, sir,
Don't tell Mama what you know!

SALLY

If you see my mummy, mum's the word!
(*During this number* SALLY *has gradually become
aware of* CLIFF. *She has sung to him, almost as if he
were the only one in the audience. At the end of the*

number SALLY *and the* GIRLS *dance off.* SALLY *re-appears soon afterward.* CLIFF *watches her intently as she goes to a "Reserved" table for two. She sits there alone for a moment. Then she picks up the phone)*

SALLY   Table number three.
(*The phone on* CLIFF's *table lights up*)

CLIFF   (*Into the phone*)   Hello?

SALLY   (*Into the phone*)   You're English!

CLIFF   I wish I were.

SALLY   American?

CLIFF   I'm sorry.

SALLY   But you *speak* English! You speak it beautifully! Will you just—keep talking—please? You can't imagine how starved I've been!

CLIFF   Okay. Let me think. (*He recites*)
The sea is calm tonight.
The tide is full, the moon lies fair
Upon the straits: —on the French coast the light
Gleams and is gone; the cliffs of England stand,
Glimmering and vast, out in the tranquil bay.
Come to the window, sweet is the night air!

SALLY   Yes—yes—don't stop—please!

CLIFF I'm afraid that's all I know. My name is Cliff Bradshaw. I come from Harrisburg, Pennsylvania. You know
where that is?

SALLY Such a beautiful language.

CLIFF Well, it's ninety miles west of Philadelphia. May I
come to your table?

SALLY It's like music! (*Pause*) Why did you stop?

CLIFF I asked you a question. I'd like to join you at your
table.

SALLY Oh. I see. Well—I'm not absolutely sure that's possible—at this time. (*A man, rather middle-aged and quite
Germanic-looking, walks up to* SALLY's *table and sits down
next to her. He looks rather irritated with her*) As a matter
of fact, I rather doubt it.
   (*The man snatches the phone out of* SALLY's *hand and
hangs it up. There is fanfare from the orchestra. The*
EMCEE *appears, dressed as Father Time*)

EMCEE Meine Damen und Herren, Mesdames et Messieurs, Ladies and Gentlemen. It is almost midnight! Hus-
bands, you have only ten seconds in which to lose your
wives! Five—four—three—two—Happy New Year!
   (*Then the stage goes black. In the darkness, there is
enormous jubilation. The* EMCEE *changes into Infant
New Year, 1930. Then a match is lit in the darkness.*

23

It is SALLY *lighting a cigarette in a long, long cigarette holder. She is sitting at* CLIFF's *table)*

SALLY   Would you recite that again—about the coast of England?

CLIFF
The sea is calm tonight,
The tide is full—
(He has a better idea. He kisses her) Happy New Year.

SALLY   I'm Sally Bowles. Are you new in Berlin?

CLIFF   Yes, I've only been here three hours.
(The man who was sitting with SALLY *has risen and is heading toward* CLIFF's *table. As he approaches,* CLIFF *sees him and starts to get up politely.* SALLY *puts her hand on* CLIFF's *arm, indicating that he should keep seated.* SALLY *glances briefly at the man—as if challenging him. The man hesitates for a moment. Then he goes away.* SALLY *turns back to* CLIFF)

SALLY   Three hours! And how long are you planning to stay?

CLIFF *(Shrugs his shoulders)*   I'm working on a novel. I'll stay till it's finished.

SALLY *(Impressed)*   You're a writer! Would I know your books?

CLIFF It's highly unlikely. Anyway, it's *book*—singular.

SALLY Was it a huge success?

CLIFF They said it showed promise.

SALLY Promise?

CLIFF (*He puts his arm around her*) Let's talk about Sally Bowles. What part of England are you from? (*No answer*) London? (*No answer*) Stratford-on-Avon? (*No answer*) Stonehenge?

SALLY Oh, Cliff, you mustn't ever ask me questions. If I want to tell you anything, I will. Why did you come to *Berlin* to do your novel?

CLIFF I'd already tried London, Rome, Venice . . .

SALLY Just looking for a place to write?

CLIFF Something to write about.

SALLY Where are you staying?
(CLIFF *shows her the card* ERNST *gave him*)

CLIFF And you, where do *you* live? A hotel?

SALLY No. Not really. It's more of a flat—actually.

CLIFF You live alone? (SALLY *shakes her head*) You think your roommate would mind if I came up for just a few minutes?

SALLY I'm afraid so. You see, Max is most terribly jealous.

CLIFF Max? (SALLY *nods again*) Your husband?

SALLY Oh, no! He's just the man I'm living with (CLIFF *looks a little surprised*)—this week. (*She studies his face*) I say—am I shocking you—talking like this?

CLIFF (*Mocking*) I say, are you trying to shock me?

SALLY Trying to . . . ? (*But she likes him for having seen through her*) You're quite right, you know. (*She kisses him; the* EMCEE *appears and signals to her. She rises*) Good luck with your writing!
(*And she is gone.* CLIFF's *phone lights up*)

CLIFF Hello?

GIRL ON PHONE (*singing*)
  Hello.
  Sitting alone like that,
  You happened to catch my eye.
  Would you like to buy a girl a drink?

CLIFF Sorry.

GIRL ON PHONE
Ach! Goodbye.
(CLIFF *exits*)

FIRST BOY (*Into phone*)
Hello

FIRST GIRL (*Into phone*)
Hello—table four is calling number nine
How are you, mister?

FIRST BOY
Danke—fine

FIRST GIRL
Sitting all alone like that,
You happened to catch my eye.
Would you like to give a girl a dance?

FIRST BOY
Yah—why not?

BOTH
Goodbye!
(*They dance*)

SECOND BOY (*Into phone*)
Hello

SECOND GIRL (*Into phone*)
Hello

THIRD BOY (*Into phone*)
    Hello

THIRD GIRL (*Into phone*)
    Hello

SECOND and THIRD GIRL
    Table seven calling number three.
    How are you, handsome?

SECOND and THIRD BOY
    You mean me?

SECOND and THIRD GIRL
    We can see you—can you see us?
    Would you like to have a dance
    The minute that the music's hot?
    Maybe we can talk it over, Ja?

THIRD BOY
    Ja!

SECOND BOY
    Of course!

SECOND and THIRD BOY
    Why not!
      (*Both couples dance*)

FOURTH and FIFTH BOY (*Into phone*)
    Alone—alone
    You shouldn't sit alone like that

Alone—alone
Not on a night like this.

ALL

Alone—alone
You shouldn't sit alone like that
Alone—alone
Not on a night like this.
(*They dance, and from different parts of the stage—
right, center, left—the dancers alternately say "Hello"*)

ALL

Sitting all alone like that,
You happened to catch my eye.

GIRLS

Would you like to buy a girl a drink?

BOYS

Would you like to buy a man a drink?

ALL

Would you like to buy a boy a drink?
(*They dance, and from different parts of the stage—
right, center, left—the dancers alternately say, "You
will," "Why not?" "Goodbye"*)

ALL   Ja!

Blackout

CLIFF's *room.* ERNST *is referring to a dictionary.* CLIFF *watches him.*

ERNST   You know what is the trouble with English? It is not like German. It is not an exact language. Or one must memorize fifty thousand words or one cannot speak it correctly.

CLIFF   *Either* one must memorize—*or* one cannot speak . . .

ERNST   Aha! *Either*—or—(ERNST *happily makes a notation in his notebook, then closes it and stands up*) The time is now finished.

CLIFF   I'm in no hurry.

ERNST   But the lesson is one hour. No? Another pupil is waiting.

CLIFF   *What* other pupil?

ERNST   No other pupil? (CLIFF *shakes his head*) Then I make a suggestion! I will telephone my lady friend. She will bring a friend for you. Elsa! A genuine flapper.

CLIFF   Not tonight, Ernst.

ERNST But you have not seen this Elsa! Hot stuff, believe me! In one minute, I guarantee, you are making a pass after her.

CLIFF A pass *at* her.

ERNST Aha!! A pass *at* her!

CLIFF The trouble is, I've *got* a date tonight.
(*He indicates his typewriter*)

ERNST A typewriter? But what can one do with a typewriter?

CLIFF Not very much—lately.

ERNST Then come with me! We make a large whoopee!

CLIFF (*Shakes his head*) For one thing, I've got a budget. And it only allows for a very small whoopee. Unfortunately.

ERNST Then you are *my* guest!

CLIFF Thanks, but . .
(*He shakes his head negatively*)

ERNST It is difficult, you know—adjusting to the idea of a *poor* American. But I tell you a secret. There is no need for this—poverty. Ja! If you are willing, I show you a most excellent way to supplement your income.

CLIFF Doing what?

ERNST   Oh—by taking very brief trips—to Paris! Perhaps a few days each time. Nothing more. But it will pay you well, extremely well.
(*There is a knock at the door*)

CLIFF   Come in.
(FRAULEIN SCHNEIDER *enters. She wears her flowered dressing gown. She is quite excited*)

FRAULEIN SCHNEIDER   Herr Bradshaw, there is a young lady to see you! A young lady in a fur coat!

CLIFF   A young lady?

FRAULEIN SCHNEIDER   Fraulein Bowles . . . ?

CLIFF   Bowles? (FRAULEIN SCHNEIDER *nods*) Ask her to come in.
(FRAULEIN SCHNEIDER *exits*)

ERNST   You are old friends—you and Fraulein Bowles? From London, perhaps . . . ?

CLIFF   From the Kit Kat Klub. Last night.

ERNST   Last night! You are some snappy operator!
(SALLY *enters wearing a fur coat, smoking a cigarette in a cigarette holder.* FRAULEIN SCHNEIDER *follows her*)

SALLY   Cliff!! (*She kisses* CLIFF) Ernst, darling! (*She kisses* ERNST. *To* CLIFF) Will you be a dear and get my bag? (*She surveys the room approvingly*) It's *lovely*, Fraulein Schneider! All these wonderful old pieces! (CLIFF *enters with her bag. To* CLIFF) Just put it anywhere. I'll unpack later.

FRAULEIN SCHNEIDER   Unpack? But Herr Bradshaw did not mention . . .

SALLY   I'll just be here temporarily.

FRAULEIN SCHNEIDER   But I am sorry. This is not possible.

SALLY (*To* CLIFF)   How much are you paying?

CLIFF   Fifty marks.

SALLY (*To* FRAULEIN SCHNEIDER)   Sixty marks?

FRAULEIN SCHNEIDER (*Shaking her head*)   It is not the money—

SALLY   Seventy?

FRAULEIN SCHNEIDER   I cannot permit—

SALLY   Eighty?
(FRAULEIN SCHNEIDER *mulls this over for a moment. She is very, very tempted*)

FRAULEIN SCHNEIDER But this room is worth one hundred marks. More than one hundred.

SALLY Eighty.

FRAULEIN SCHNEIDER Eighty-five! (*They shake hands*) And now—please make yourself cosy—*Frau* Bradshaw.
(FRAULEIN SCHNEIDER *exits.* ERNST *looks at his watch*)

ERNST (*To* CLIFF) Such a to-do! I will see you Friday for the next lesson. But I tell you something: I think I am taking from you the *wrong kind* of lessons.
(ERNST *exits.* SALLY, *still in her fur coat, collapses onto the bed*)

CLIFF Sally, now what's this all about?

SALLY Did you guess I was terrified?

CLIFF Were you?

SALLY What if you'd—thrown me out? Can you imagine how *that* would feel—being thrown out twice in one day?

CLIFF You mean—Max . . . ?

SALLY Dear Max. And you know whose fault it was? (*She points at* CLIFF) If you hadn't come to the Kit Kat Klub —and been so dreadfully attractive—and recited poetry— (*She suddenly sits up*) You know what I'd love? A spot of gin.

CLIFF Gin?

SALLY   You've *got* some? I mean—I think one *must*.

CLIFF   No, I don't have any . . .

SALLY   Oh, well, Prairie Oysters, then.

CLIFF   Prairie Oysters?

SALLY   I practically live on them. It's just a raw egg whooshed around in some Worcestershire sauce. It's heaven for a hangover.

CLIFF   I haven't got a hangover. (SALLY *takes eggs, salt, pepper and Worcestershire sauce out of her coat pocket.* CLIFF *watches her*) That's quite a coat.

SALLY   It should be. It cost me all I had. Little did I dream how soon I'd be unemployed.

CLIFF   What about your job at the Klub?

SALLY   Well, that's rather complicated. You see, one of the owners of the Klub . . .

CLIFF   Dear Max?

SALLY   You're divinely intuitive! I do hope I'm not going to fall madly in love with you. Are you in the theatre in any way? (CLIFF *shakes his head*) Then you're safe—more or less. Though I do believe a woman can't be a truly great

35

actress till she's had several passionate affairs—and had her
heart broken. (*Manufacturing the Prairie Oysters,* SALLY
breaks the eggs on this line) I should have let Ernst pay my
cab fare. He's got all that money from Paris.

CLIFF   From Paris?

SALLY   He smuggles it in for some political party.

CLIFF   Ernst is in politics?

SALLY   You didn't know? He goes to Paris about once a
month and brings back pots of money.

CLIFF   He has to smuggle it in?

SALLY   It's terribly dangerous. But Ernst is so resourceful.
He's discovered the Customs people almost never open the
bags of non-Germans. So, just before the border, he finds
some innocent-looking Englishman—or American . . .
        (*She completes the Prairie Oysters*)

CLIFF   It's hard to imagine an American *that* gullible.
        (SALLY *hands him his drink. She toasts*)

SALLY   Hals and beinbruch. It means neck and leg break.
It's supposed to stop it happening. Though I doubt it does.

CLIFF (*Toasting*)   Look—it's about time we—

SALLY   Drink!
        (SALLY *drinks her Prairie Oyster. Then* CLIFF *sips his*)

CLIFF It's amazing! You know what this tastes like? Peppermint!

SALLY Oh—well, it's your toothbrush glass. I should have rinsed it. (SALLY *wanders over to the writing table. She picks up a book*) This is your novel! (*She opens it*) It's in German! (*She looks at the cover*) Mein Kampf?

CLIFF It's not my novel. I thought I should know *something* about German politics.

SALLY Why? You're an American! You know, I've never *known* a novelist. Will I be allowed to watch you work? I promise to be incredibly quiet . . .

CLIFF I don't think I can write with someone else—on the premises.

SALLY But I'm hardly noticeable—really. (*Imploring*) I'll go out when you're writing—take long invigorating walks!

CLIFF In the middle of the night? And there's another thing: I'm not a prude. At least, I don't think I'm a prude. No—no—I've got work to do. I could never explain this arrangement. It's too peculiar.

SALLY Peculiar? No, not in the least!
        (*Spoken, but the music is playing*)
    I think people are people. I really do, Cliff,
        don't you?
    I don't think they should be made to apologize
        for anything they do.

For example, if I paint my fingernails green—
And it happens I do paint them green—
Well, if someone should ask me why,
I think it's pretty.
I think it's pretty, *that's* what I reply.
So, if anyone should ask about you and me one day,
You have two alternatives:
You can either say: "Yes, it's true we're living in
delicious sin,"
Or you can simply tell them the truth, and say . . .
    (SALLY *sings*)
I met this perfectly marvelous girl
In this perfectly wonderful place
As I lifted a glass to the start of a marvelous year.
Before you knew it she called on the phone, inviting.
Next moment I was no longer alone,
But sat reciting some perfectly beautiful verse
In my charming American style.
How I dazzled her senses was truly no less than a
    crime.
Now I've this perfectly marvelous girl
In my perfectly beautiful room,
And we're living together and having a marvelous time.

CLIFF   Sally, I'm afraid it wouldn't work. You're much too
distracting.

SALLY   Distracting? No, inspiring! (*She sings*)
    She tells me perfectly marvelous tales
    Of her thrillingly scandalous life
    Which I'll probably use as a chapter or two
      in my book.

And since my stay in Berlin was to force
Creation,
What luck to fall on a fabulous source
Of stimulation.
And perfectly marvelous too
Is her perfect agreement to be
Just as still as a mouse when I'm giving my novel
    a whirl.
Yes, I've a highly agreeable life
In my perfectly beautiful room,
With my nearly invisible,
Perfectly marvelous girl.

(*There is a noise at the door*) Oh, it's the taxi man! (*The door bursts open, and there is the taxi man with a mountain of luggage*) Hello, taxi man. Just put them anywhere. I'll unpack later. (CLIFF, *a little dazed, points to all the baggage*) Things *do* accumulate. I'll throw most of it away—tomorrow! I promise! (CLIFF *helps the taxi man bring in the bags.* SALLY *starts counting the pieces*) One—two—three—four—five— (*She gives up*) There's really not much point in counting. I never remember how many they're supposed to be. (*To* CLIFF) Can you let me have three marks? That includes the tip. (CLIFF *hands her a bill*) Thank you. (SALLY *hands the bill to the taxi man, who tips his cap and exits. There is a pause*) So quite seriously, Cliff—please may I stay?

CLIFF Sally, I can't afford—

SALLY Only for a day or two—please?

CLIFF (*singing*)
    I met this truly remarkable girl

In this really incredible town,
And she's skillfully managed to talk her way
    into my room.

SALLY Oh, Cliff!

CLIFF
  I have a terrible feeling I've said a dumb thing;
  Besides, I've only got one narrow bed.

SALLY
  We'll think of something.

CLIFF
  And now this wild, unpredictable girl

SALLY
  And this perfectly beautiful man

BOTH
  Will be living together and having a marvelous time.
  (They are in each other's arms as the lights fade)

Scene 6

The EMCEE *appears, followed by two sexy* LADIES.

EMCEE   Everybody in Berlin has a perfectly marvelous room-mate. Some people have two people!

FIRST LADY (*singing*)
   Beedle-dee-deedle-dee-dee

SECOND LADY
   Beedle-dee-deedle-dee-dee

EMCEE
   Beedle-dee-deedle-dee
   Deedle-dee-deedle-dee-dee!

LADIES
   Beedle-dee-deedle-dee-dee

EMCEE
   Two ladies

LADIES
   Beedle-dee-deedle-dee-dee

EMCEE
   Two ladies

LADIES
Beedle-dee-deedle-dee-dee

EMCEE
And I'm the only man, Ja!

LADIES
Beedle-dee-deedle-dee-dee

EMCEE
I like it.

LADIES
Beedle-dee-deedle-dee-dee

EMCEE
They like it.

LADIES
Beedle-dee-deedle-dee-dee

EMCEE
This two for one.
Beedle-dee-deedle-dee-dee

LADIES
Two ladies

EMCEE
Beedle-dee-deedle-dee-dee

LADIES
Two ladies

EMCEE
Beedle-dee-deedle-dee-dee

LADIES
And he's the only man!

EMCEE
Ja!

ALL
Beedle-dee-deedle-dee-dee

FIRST LADY
He likes it.

EMCEE
Beedle-dee-deedle-dee-dee

SECOND LADY
We like it.

EMCEE
Beedle-dee-deedle-dee-dee

LADIES
This two for one.

FIRST LADY
I do the cooking.

SECOND LADY
  And I make the bed.

EMCEE
  I go out daily to earn our daily bread.
  But we've one thing in common—

FIRST LADY
  He!

EMCEE
  She

SECOND LADY
  And me!

FIRST LADY
  The key!

EMCEE
  Beedle-dee

SECOND LADY
  The key!

EMCEE
  Beedle-dee
  The key!

LADIES
  Beedle-deedle-deedle-dee
  (*They dance*)

44

EMCEE

We switch partners daily
To play as we please.

LADIES

Twosie beats onesie,

EMCEE

But nothing beats threes.
I sleep in the middle.

FIRST LADY

I'm left.

SECOND LADY

And I'm right.

EMCEE

But there's room on the bottom if you drop in some
night.

LADIES

Beedle-dee-deedle-dee-dee

EMCEE

Two ladies
Beedle-dee-deedle-dee-dee

LADIES

Two ladies
Beedle-dee-deedle-dee-dee
And he's the only man, Ja!

ALL
>Beedle-dee-deedle-dee-dee

EMCEE
>I like it.

ALL
>Beedle-dee-deedle-dee-dee

EMCEE
>We like it.

ALL
>Beedle-dee-deedle-dee-dee
>This two for one
>Beedle-dee-deedle-dee-deedle-dee-deedle-dee-dee
>>(*They exit*)

Blackout

FRAULEIN SCHNEIDER's *living room. It is dominated by a large sofa which nestles between two hideous end tables. An old gramophone lurks in the background.*

Doors lead from the living room to the rooms of FRAULEIN KOST *and* HERR SCHULTZ—*also to the bedroom of* FRAULEIN SCHNEIDER. *A large double door leads outside. A hallway extends offstage, leading to still more rooms.*

As the lights come up FRAULEIN KOST *is entering through the double door with a* GERMAN SAILOR. *He pinches her. She screams. And* FRAULEIN SCHNEIDER *zooms out of her room to accost them.*

FRAULEIN SCHNEIDER   That sailor! Out of my house!

FRAULEIN KOST   That sailor—dear lady—is my brother!

FRAULEIN SCHNEIDER   Out! Out! Out!
　　(*The* GERMAN SAILOR *exits through the double door*)

FRAULEIN KOST   Wait! Wait! How dare you! You think it is easy—finding a sailor? This was only my second one since New Year's. And what is it now? April!

FRAULEIN SCHNEIDER   Your second? Your *second*? You think I do not know what goes on here? Sailors—all the time. In —out—in—out! God only knows what the neighbors must

think I have here—a battleship? (*Outraged*) Fraulein Kost,
I give you warning! One sailor more—I call the police!

FRAULEIN KOST   And if I cannot pay the rent?

FRAULEIN SCHNEIDER   The rent is due each Friday—as
always.

FRAULEIN KOST   No sailors. No rent. I move.

FRAULEIN SCHNEIDER   Move?

FRAULEIN KOST   Move!

FRAULEIN SCHNEIDER (*Upset*)   And what am I supposed to
do with your room? Out of the blue—she tells me "I move"!
Is that gratitude? Only last week I gave you another new
mattress!

FRAULEIN KOST   All right! I will leave the end of the week—
since you insist.

FRAULEIN SCHNEIDER   *I* insist? *You* insist!

FRAULEIN KOST   And what about the sailors?

FRAULEIN SCHNEIDER   The sailors? (*She mulls it over and
reaches a decision*) Fraulein Kost—if you wish to continue
living here, do not let me *catch* you bringing in any more
sailors? You understand?

48

FRAULEIN KOST (*Haughtily*)   Very well. So it is the same as always.
(*She goes into her room and closes the door*)

FRAULEIN SCHNEIDER   It is *not* the same as always! (*She knocks on* FRAULEIN KOST's *door*) Fraulein Kost! You hear me? I have put my foot down! (*She knocks again*) Fraulein Kost! Fraulein Kost!
(*Meanwhile,* HERR SCHULTZ *has emerged from his room, wearing his best suit and carrying a brown paper bag*)

SCHULTZ   Fraulein Schneider—Good evening!
(FRAULEIN SCHNEIDER *sees* HERR SCHULTZ. *She quickly and adroitly switches from AC to DC*)

FRAULEIN SCHNEIDER   Herr Schultz! Such a surprise!

SCHULTZ   You are occupied?

FRAULEIN SCHNEIDER   No. No. Free as a bird. Please forgive my appearance.
(*She indicates her dress. If necessary, she could wear it to the opera—and she knows it*)

SCHULTZ   But it is most becoming.

FRAULEIN SCHNEIDER   Thank you.

SCHULTZ (*Indicating the paper bag*)   I have brought you a little something from the shop.

FRAULEIN SCHNEIDER   *Another* little something?
(HERR SCHULTZ *hands her the bag*)

SCHULTZ   With my compliments.
(FRAULEIN SCHNEIDER *feels the bag*)

FRAULEIN SCHNEIDER   So heavy! But what can it be? Pears?
(*She shakes her head merrily*) Last Wednesday you brought
me pears. And such pears! Apples, possibly? (*She rejects
the idea*) Friday was apples.

SCHULTZ (*Nods*)   Friday was apples.

FRAULEIN SCHNEIDER   So I cannot guess . . .

SCHULTZ   Then open!
(FRAULEIN SCHNEIDER *peers into the bag*)

FRAULEIN SCHNEIDER   Herr Schultz! Can I believe what I
see? (HERR SCHULTZ *nods proudly*) But this is—too much
to accept. So rare—so costly—so luxurious. (*She sings*)
   If you bought me diamonds,
   If you bought me pearls,
   If you bought me roses like some other gents
   Might bring to other girls,
   It couldn't please me more
   Than the gift I see—
   (*She takes a large pineapple out of the bag*)
   A pineapple for me!

SCHULTZ (*singing*)
   If, in your emotion,
   You began to sway,

50

Went to get some air,
Or grabbed a chair
To keep from fainting dead away,
It couldn't please me more
Than to see you cling
To the pineapple I bring.

BOTH
Ah, ah, ah, ah, ah, ah, ah, ah

FRAULEIN SCHNEIDER
I can hear Hawaiian breezes blow.

BOTH
Ah, ah, ah, ah, ah, ah

SCHULTZ
It's from California.

FRAULEIN SCHNEIDER
Even so,
How am I to thank you?

SCHULTZ
Kindly let it pass.

FRAULEIN SCHNEIDER
Would you like a slice?

SCHULTZ
That might be nice,
But frankly, it would give me gas.

FRAULEIN SCHNEIDER
Then we shall leave it here—
Not to eat, but see.

BOTH
A pineapple

FRAULEIN SCHNEIDER
For me!

SCHULTZ
From me!

BOTH
Ah, ah, ah, ah, ah ah
Ah, ah, ah, ah, ah ah
(*They dance*)

FRAULEIN SCHNEIDER But you must not bring me any more pineapples! Do you hear? It is not proper. It is a gift a young man would present to his lady love. It makes me blush!

SCHULTZ But there is no one—no one in all Berlin—who is more deserving! If I could, I would fill your entire room with pineapples!
(FRAULEIN SCHNEIDER *is quite surprised by this.* HERR SCHULTZ *is even more surprised. He had no idea he was going to say it*)

BOTH (*singing*)
A pineapple . . .

SCHULTZ
For you!

FRAULEIN SCHNEIDER
From you!

BOTH
Ah, ah, ah, ah, ah, ah
(*The music continues*)

FRAULEIN SCHNEIDER I think I will lie down for a few minutes. My head is spinning.

SCHULTZ Good evening, Fraulein.

FRAULEIN SCHNEIDER Good evening, Herr Schultz. (*They shake hands.* FRAULEIN SCHNEIDER *opens her bedroom door, then turns to* HERR SCHULTZ) I am—over whelmed!
(*She goes in and closes the door. The music ends.* HERR SCHULTZ *is all atingle. He makes a decision. He is about to knock on* FRAULEIN SCHNEIDER's *door when suddenly he hears a sound. He jumps back from the door. He kneels down as if looking for something.* FRAULEIN KOST *opens her door and comes out. She wonders why* HERR SCHULTZ *is so far from his own door*)

FRAULEIN KOST Good evening, Herr Schultz.

HERR SCHULTZ Good evening, Fraulein Kost. I am looking for—I think I dropped—a small coin—a groschen. It rolled this way.

FRAULEIN KOST You're looking for a groschen? (*Meaning-fully*) I'm looking for two marks. *on his face*
(FRAULEIN KOST *exits.* HERR SCHULTZ *goes again to* FRAULEIN SCHNEIDER's *door. He knocks. Immediately the door swings open. He swiftly enters. The door closes*)

Blackout

A group of WAITERS *are seen on the spiral staircase. They are handsome, well-scrubbed, idealistic. The* EMCEE *is seated stage right.*

WAITERS (*singing*)
    The sun on the meadow is summery warm,
    The stag in the forest runs free,
    But gather together to greet the storm,
    Tomorrow belongs to me.

    The branch of the linden is leafy and green,
    The Rhine gives its gold to the sea,
    But somewhere a glory awaits unseen,
    Tomorrow belongs to me.

    (*The* EMCEE *joins the* WAITERS *in song*)

Oh, Fatherland, Fatherland, show us the sign
Your children have waited to see.
The morning will come when the world is mine,
Tomorrow belongs to me.
    (*The* WAITERS *disappear upstage, leaving a leering* EMCEE *alone as the lights dim*)

CLIFF's *room.* SALLY's *things are everywhere—on the floor, bulging out of the drawers, peeking out of the closets.*

CLIFF *is at the writing desk, typing.* SALLY *enters with groceries, kisses* CLIFF, *takes off her fur coat, and comes over to see what he is writing.*

CLIFF   It's not the novel. It's a letter to my mother—thanking her for the check.

SALLY   It finally arrived!
(CLIFF *indicates the check from his mother*)

CLIFF   Everyone at home's very thrilled the novel's going so well. Any day now they're expecting to see it in the bookstores.

SALLY   Oh, Cliff—

CLIFF   I may not be a good novelist, but I'm a very good liar. And I write a hell of a letter.

SALLY   It's my fault. If I weren't always dragging you off to party after party . . .

CLIFF   But I *like* those parties. The truth is, I like this whole city. It's so tacky and terrible—and everyone's having such

56

a great time. ~~If this were~~ a movie, you know what would ~~happen?~~ A volcano would erupt—or there'd be a tidal wave . . .

SALLY   Maybe you should write for films! And I'll star in them! Oh, Cliff—wouldn't that be heaven!

CLIFF   Heaven! Just as soon as I finish the novel.

SALLY   There must be *something* to write about?

CLIFF   Or someone? Sally Bowles? Who would ever believe it?

SALLY   You're right—I'm much too strange and extraordinary! Much! And much too distracting . . .

CLIFF   Distracting? Nonsense! What about Venice? What about Rome? There was no Sally Bowles then—and no novel either. I was just drifting . . .

SALLY   And now you're sleepwalking. Is that better?

CLIFF   Sleepwalking? Who said that?

SALLY   *You* did. Last night.

CLIFF   I was drunk last night. Anyway—I said it was *possible* I was sleepwalking. And—if I am—who cares? What's the point in opening my eyes? (*Singing*)

Why should I wake up?
This dream is going so well.
When you're enchanted,
Why break the spell?
Drifting in this euphoric state,
Morning can wait.
Let it come late.
Why should I wake up?
Why waste a drop of the wine?
Don't I adore you?
And aren't you mine?
Maybe I'll someday be lonely again.
But why should I wake up till then?

SALLY Even so, Cliff—I've always said: When you want me
to go, I'll go . . . even this very minute. I've never stayed so
long with anyone.

CLIFF Let's not talk about that! (*Singing*)
Drifting in this euphoric state,
Morning can wait.
Let it come late.
Why should I wake up?
Why waste a drop of the wine?
Don't I adore you?
And aren't you mine?
Maybe I'll someday be lonely again.
But why should I wake up,
Why should I wake up till then?
There's a letter for you from England.

SALLY England?
(*She is afraid to take the letter from him*)

CLIFF It won't bite.

SALLY Don't be too sure. (*She picks up the letter and looks at the envelope*) It's from Sybil! She's just a mad girl I used to go to school with! We were utterly wild—smoking cigarettes and not wearing bloomers! Our parents predicted we'd both come to a bad end—and the truth is—*she did.*

CLIFF Why? What happened?

SALLY She met this absolutely dreary boy and fell hopelessly in love with him and married him and now they have two children. (*She indicates the letter*) Probably another one on the way. (*Pause*) It looks as if *everybody's* got one on the way.
(*There is a pause.* CLIFF *looks at* SALLY)

CLIFF What? Are you sure? (SALLY *nods*) How long have you known?

SALLY Oh—a day or two.

CLIFF Good God! How do you feel about it?

SALLY I don't know, Cliff. I was going to ask how *you* feel.

CLIFF Terrible! How else could I feel? I haven't got a dime! I haven't got—anything!

SALLY It does seem—a bad idea. Good heavens, if you find
me distracting—can you imagine a baby!

CLIFF It's just not the time.

SALLY I think you're perfectly right. So what shall we do?
(*Pause*) The usual thing? (*No answer*) Cliff . . . ?

CLIFF It's not the first time—is it?

SALLY Oh, Cliff—remember—you mustn't ever ask me
questions! The truth is, I should never have told you about
the baby. But I thought if *you* didn't mind—perhaps *I*
wouldn't mind. It might even have been rather—nice. But
now we know where we stand. The subject is closed.

CLIFF Will I ever be able to figure you out?

SALLY After all, it's as much my fault as yours.

CLIFF You are the world's craziest girl. It's no easy matter,
you know, being in love with the world's craziest girl. (*They
kiss*) Who says I'd be a terrible father?

SALLY But is it the time?

CLIFF Yes! It's time. Time I got a job.

SALLY What about your novel?

CLIFF If I'm going to be a writer, I'll be a writer—in the evening, in the morning, in the bathtub. This might be the best thing that ever happened to me.

SALLY And I'll go back to the Kit Kat Klub!

CLIFF Oh, no! (*There is a knock on the door*) Come in!
(*The door opens and* ERNST LUDWIG *is there*)

ERNST Clifford—Sally— (*They shake hands*) I do not wish to intrude, but I have urgent business.

SALLY Would you like something? A drink?

ERNST Only if you will join me.
(CLIFF *nods.* SALLY *starts pouring three glasses of whiskey*)

CLIFF (*To* ERNST) What's on your mind?

ERNST You remember—I mentioned the possibility of an occasional business trip to Paris . . . (CLIFF *nods*) If you are interested—I think—in the next few days . . .

CLIFF What would I have to do?

ERNST It is so very simple. You go to an address I will give you—you pick up a small briefcase—you bring it back to Berlin. And then I pay you seventy-five marks!

61

SALLY   Seventy-five marks! Cliff—it's a gift from heaven!

ERNST   And I promise you are giving help to a very good cause.

CLIFF   Well, whatever it is, please don't tell me. I don't want to know.

ERNST   As you wish. But you will go?

SALLY   Of course he will!

ERNST   Clifford?

CLIFF   You see how it is? And we're not even married yet.

ERNST   Married! But such a surprise! My congratulations! Sally, congratulations. And when is the wedding to be? (CLIFF *shrugs his shoulders*)

CLIFF   We haven't decided yet. This all just happened *today*.

ERNST   Today?

SALLY   Of course. We only *found out* today.
(ERNST *looks at* SALLY *very quizzically.* CLIFF *quickly raises his glass of whiskey*)

CLIFF　That we're going to be rich! Here—drink up! I mean, Prost!

(SALLY *and* ERNST *raise their glasses*)

SALLY, ERNST and CLIFF　Prosit!
(*They drink as the lights fade*)

At the top of the spiral staircase, the EMCEE *appears. He wears expensive clothes and flashy jewelry.*

EMCEE   Prosit! You see? There's more than one way to make money! (*He sings*)
　　My father needs money,
　　My uncle needs money,
　　My mother is thin as a reed.
　　But me, I'm sitting pretty—
　　I've got all the money I need.

　　My dearest friend Fritzy
　　Is out of his wits, he
　　Has four starving children to feed.
　　But me, I'm sitting pretty—
　　I've got all the money I need.

　　I know my little cousin Eric
　　Has his creditors hysterical,
　　And also Cousin Herman
　　Had to pawn his mother's ermine,
　　And my sister and my brother
　　Took to hocking one another, too.

　　But I've got some talents
　　Which build up my balance,
　　So even my bankers agreed
　　That me, I'm sitting pretty—
　　I've got all the money I need.

You wonder where I get my money? I have something to sell. Love! For all tastes! From all over! Meet Olga, my Russian ruble! (*A beautiful* RUSSIAN GIRL *enters, her bosom covered with rubles. The* EMCEE *helps himself to a few rubles.*) The Russian ruble will never collapse! Sushi, my Japanese yen! (*A stunning* JAPANESE GIRL *enters, a yen on each breast. The* EMCEE *takes one yen*) I have one yen. (*He takes the other*) I have two yen. (*He turns to the audience*) You have a yen? My French franc! Voilà! (*A gorgeous* FRENCH GIRL *enters with a French franc in her hand, which she gives the* EMCEE) And now—Ladies and Gentlemen —My American buck! (*A beautiful* AMERICAN GIRL *enters, an American dollar in the beak of the eagle headdress she wears. He take the dollar and sings*)

I know my little cousin Eric
Has his creditors hysterical,
And also Cousin Herman
Had to pawn his mother's ermine,
And my sister and my brother
Took to hocking one another, too.

But, I'm not a nincompoop.
I've got an income you
Put in the bank to accrue.
Yes, me, I'm sitting pretty—
Life is pretty sitting with you!
(*They dance*)
And now, Brünnhilde, my German mark—you can't keep that girl down!
(*She rises from behind the piano and "flies" straight up in the air. She poses for a brief moment, and as she is descending, he hits the gong that is between her legs*)

ALL (*singing*)
    Life is pretty sitting with,
    Pretty sitting with,
    Pretty sitting with you!

Blackout

FRAULEIN SCHNEIDER's *living room is empty. Then*
FRAULEIN KOST's *door opens slowly.* FRAULEIN KOST *looks out.*
All seems to be clear. A SAILOR *emerges.*
Just at this moment, FRAULEIN SCHNEIDER *opens her bed-*
room door. The two ladies spot each other.

FRAULEIN KOST   All right! There is no need to say it! I know
it by heart already! (*The* SAILOR *exits. For some strange*
reason, FRAULEIN SCHNEIDER *says nothing*) So no lectures
—please—about sailors! They are just lonesome, patriotic
boys! I have a duty! (FRAULEIN SCHNEIDER *still says nothing.*
She looks vaguely uncomfortable. Inexplicably, FRAULEIN
SCHNEIDER *goes back into her bedroom and closes the door.*
FRAULEIN KOST *is quite surprised. She goes into her room.*
A moment later, FRAULEIN KOST *opens her door and another*
SAILOR *emerges. As she is about to close her door,* FRAULEIN
SCHNEIDER's *door opens and* HERR SCHULTZ *peeks out.*
FRAULEIN KOST *sees him but he doesn't see her. Both doors*
close. After a while, FRAULEIN SCHNEIDER's *door opens and*
HERR SCHULTZ *starts out, followed by* FRAULEIN SCHNEIDER.
At this point, FRAULEIN KOST *opens her door and she comes*
out—very brazenly—followed by yet another SAILOR. *For*
FRAULEIN SCHNEIDER's *benefit,* FRAULEIN KOST *hugs and*
kisses the SAILOR *at great length*) Goodnight, Karl.

SAILOR (*Correcting her*)   Fritz.

FRAULEIN KOST   Fritz—you must be sure to come back again
soon. At any time. (*Taking money from him*) Bring your
friends. (*The* SAILOR *exits.* FRAULEIN KOST *waltzes up to*

FRAULEIN SCHNEIDER) Ah—good evening, Fraulein Schneider. A busy evening, no? I see we are—after all—sisters under the skin.

SCHULTZ   Fraulein Kost!

FRAULEIN KOST   Yes?

SCHULTZ   This fine lady is *not* your sister! She has just honored me by consenting to give me her hand in marriage!

FRAULEIN KOST (*Really amazed*)   Marriage!

SCHULTZ   We marry in—three weeks.

FRAULEIN KOST   Three weeks!

SCHULTZ   So a little respect for the future Frau Schultz—if you please!

FRAULEIN KOST   Ja! Ja! Frau Schultz?
          (FRAULEIN KOST—*chastened—exits into her room*)

FRAULEIN SCHNEIDER   Herr Schultz. You were—supreme.

SCHULTZ   But what else could I do?

FRAULEIN SCHNEIDER   Such a magnificent lie—to preserve my reputation.

SCHULTZ   But why did I say three weeks? Why not three months? Three years? This way she will find out the truth so quickly. Unless—

FRAULEIN SCHNEIDER   Unless?

SCHULTZ   Unless what?

FRAULEIN SCHNEIDER   You said "unless"!

SCHULTZ   But it is foolish! I mean—after all—who would have *me?* An elderly widower—with gray hair—and heartburn—and a little fruit . . .

FRAULEIN SCHNEIDER   Am I such a bargain then? An unbeautiful spinster with a few rooms to let—poorly furnished.

SCHULTZ   I work fourteen hours a day.

FRAULEIN SCHNEIDER   I do my own scrubbing.

SCHULTZ   My right leg bothers me.

FRAULEIN SCHNEIDER   I have such palpitations.

SCHULTZ   I'm not a well man.

FRAULEIN SCHNEIDER   Am I a well woman?

SCHULTZ   What are we talking about? We're *alive!* And what good is it—alone? So if you would even consider—marriage . . . ?
(*There is a long pause*)

FRAULEIN SCHNEIDER   I will consider it.

SCHULTZ   But take your time, by all means. No hurry.

FRAULEIN SCHNEIDER   Yes. I will consider it. (*They shake hands*) But this much I can tell you. You have good reason to be very, very optimistic.
(FRAULEIN SCHNEIDER *goes to her room.* HERR SCHULTZ, *shaken, sings*)

SCHULTZ
How the world can change,
It can change like that
Due to one little word—
Married.

See a palace rise
From a two-room flat
Due to one little word—
Married.

And the old despair
That was often there
Suddenly ceases to be.
For you wake one day,
Look around and say,

Somebody wonderful
Married me.
(*The lights come up in* FRAULEIN SCHNEIDER's *bedroom. Through the wall, we see* FRAULEIN SCHNEIDER *sitting thoughtfully on the edge of her bed*)

FRAULEIN SCHNEIDER (*singing*)
How the world can change,
It can change like that
Due to one little word—

SCHULTZ and FRAULEIN SCHNEIDER
Married.

FRAULEIN SCHNEIDER
See a palace rise
From a two-room flat
Due to one little word—

SCHULTZ and FRAULEIN SCHNEIDER
Married.

FRAULEIN SCHNEIDER
And the old despair
That was often there
Suddenly ceases to be.

SCHULTZ and FRAULEIN SCHNEIDER
For you wake one day,
Look around and say,

SCHULTZ
Somebody wonderful,

FRAULEIN SCHNEIDER
   Somebody wonderful

SCHULTZ and FRAULEIN SCHNEIDER
   Married me.
      (*The light goes out in* FRAULEIN SCHNEIDER'S *bedroom. She comes out of her door and back to the living room*)

FRAULEIN SCHNEIDER   Herr Schultz—I have considered your proposal.

SCHULTZ   So quickly?

FRAULEIN SCHNEIDER (*Nods*)   I can think of no arguments *against* it. And so—if you still desire me—I am yours.

SCHULTZ   If I desire . . . ? *If?* I must tell someone the good news! I must tell everyone! Good news! Good news! (*He rushes to one of the doors and starts knocking on it*) Is anyone there? I have news! Exciting news!

FRAULEIN SCHNEIDER   But that is your own door!

SCHULTZ   Oh! Good news! Good news! Come and hear!
      (SALLY *enters through the double door*)

SALLY   What's going on?

SCHULTZ   Fraulein Sally! Good news! Fraulein Schneider and I are to be married!

72

SALLY   Married! How wonderful! It's in the air! It must be!

SCHULTZ   I am so happy! (*He sits down*) I never thought
—I never thought I would be so fortunate.

SALLY   I've got the most perfect idea! When Cliff comes back
from Paris, we're giving you an engagement party!

FRAULEIN SCHNEIDER   Engagement party? For two old people
—it is not suitable.

SCHULTZ   *What* old people? I do not see any old people!
But *I* will give the party! I will give it at my shop! And there
will be music—dancing.

FRAULEIN SCHNEIDER   And who will dance? How many
people do we know?

SALLY   I'll do the inviting! I know lots of people!

FRAULEIN SCHNEIDER   I still think it is foolish—this party—
a waste of money!

SCHULTZ   Have you ever had an engagement party?

FRAULEIN SCHNEIDER   Of course not.

SCHULTZ   And neither have I. So—I ask you—what are we
waiting for? It's *time!*
　　　(*The lights fade, except for a spot on* FRAULEIN
　　　SCHNEIDER's *gramophone as* FRAULEIN SCHNEIDER *and*
　　　HERR SCHULTZ *waltz off*)

The lights come up on HERR SCHULTZ's fruit shop—all decorated for the party, which is in full swing. Prominent among the guests are the performers and GIRL ORCHESTRA from the Kit Kat Klub.

CLIFF enters—carrying his suitcase and ERNST's briefcase. SALLY kisses him.

SALLY Cliff! Was Paris divine?

CLIFF Divine.

SALLY (Indicating the briefcase) Was there any trouble?

CLIFF No. But I'll be happy to get rid of it. Is Ernst here?

SALLY Not yet. (CLIFF takes off his overcoat and puts the briefcase with it on a counter) Come see the lovely gift we're giving Fraulein Schneider and Herr Schultz.
(CLIFF embraces FRAULEIN SCHNEIDER)

CLIFF Fraulein . . . (Asking HERR SCHULTZ's approval to kiss her) May I? (HERR SCHULTZ nods. CLIFF kisses FRAULEIN SCHNEIDER) Congratulations.

SALLY (To FRAULEIN SCHNEIDER) Now open our present. Be careful.
(FRAULEIN SCHNEIDER undoes the ribbon from a large white gift box.)

FRAULEIN SCHNEIDER   Ah—Herr Schultz—look! Crystal!

SALLY   Cut crystal. It's for fruit.   *symbolism*

FRAULEIN SCHNEIDER   Beautiful.

SCHULTZ   Thank you. And I will keep it filled. I promise—
as long as we live—this bowl will not be empty.
(*Everyone applauds. The door opens and* FRAULEIN
KOST *enters*)

FRAULEIN KOST   Fraulein Schneider—I am welcome?

FRAULEIN SCHNEIDER   Fraulein Kost—forgive me! I did not
invite you. But only because I know you work in the
evening.

FRAULEIN KOST   Tonight I am free.

FRAULEIN SCHNEIDER (*Aside*)   I should live that long.
(*She indicates that* FRAULEIN KOST *is welcome.* FRAU-
LEIN KOST *points to the door*)

FRAULEIN KOST   My cousins?

FRAULEIN SCHNEIDER   From Hamburg? (FRAULEIN KOST
nods) In!

FRAULEIN KOST   My cousins! (*Three* SAILORS *burst in. They
find girls to dance with.* FRAULEIN KOST *stops one of them*)
Otto..

SAILOR (*Correcting her*) Rudy

FRAULEIN KOST   Rudy—it's Fraulein Schneider's party. If you want to dance—dance with her!

FRAULEIN SCHNEIDER   No—no.

FRAULEIN KOST   Dance with her, Otto!

SAILOR   Rudy! (*He comes up to* FRAULEIN SCHNEIDER) It is my pleasure, Fraulein.

FRAULEIN SCHNEIDER   But I do not . . . And you are so young . . . It is out of the question. Unthinkable—absolutely unthinkable. Absolutely.
(*And she begins to dance with him—the fruit-shop dance. At the end of the dance,* ERNST LUDWIG *enters. He has a swastika armband on his overcoat*)

ERNST   Clifford—Sally.

SALLY   Ernst!

ERNST   You have the briefcase? (CLIFF *points to the swastika armband*) Oh—I come direct from the meeting. (ERNST *takes his overcoat off. He is wearing a business suit*) I am sorry, Clifford—since you did not wish to know my politics. However—the briefcase, please. You have it?
(CLIFF *hesitates.* SALLY *hands it to* ERNST)

SALLY   Here it is.

CLIFF (*To* ERNST)   You said it was a good cause—if I remember correctly.

ERNST   And so it is! Our party will be the builders of the new Germany. And you are helping! So—for you— (ERNST *extends an envelope to* CLIFF. CLIFF *doesn't take it*) Something is wrong?
      (SALLY *takes the envelope*)

SALLY   No. Of course not. Thank you, Ernst.

CLIFF (*To* ERNST)   I've been reading your leader's book . . .

ERNST   Ah, yes. *Mein Kampf.*

CLIFF   Have you read it?

ERNST   Certainly!

CLIFF   Then I don't understand. I mean—that man is out of his mind. It's right there on every page . . .

ERNST   Clifford—this is not the time nor the place for such a discussion. Perhaps you would never understand. At any rate—now I find myself a flapper—I enjoy the party. (ERNST *leaves* CLIFF *and* SALLY. *He goes up to* FRAULEIN SCHNEIDER) Fraulein Schneider—I wish you much happiness!

FRAULEIN SCHNEIDER   Thank you.

ERNST I am sorry to be late, but there was a meeting. An important business meeting.

FRAULEIN SCHNEIDER One does what one must.

ERNST But now I look forward to a most delightful evening. (ERNST *wanders off—looking for a flapper.* HERR SCHULTZ, *carrying a bottle of schnapps and some glasses, comes up to* FRAULEIN SCHNEIDER)

SCHULTZ Schnapps?

FRAULEIN SCHNEIDER You've had enough.
(HERR SCHULTZ *watches the dancing couples admiringly*)

SCHULTZ Beautiful dancing! Beautiful! (*He suddenly notes two boys dancing together. He looks around to see if anyone else has noticed.*) All right! Enough dancing! Enough! No more dancing!

FRAULEIN SCHNEIDER But why?

SCHULTZ No more dancing! (*The music stops. The dancers stop*) Sit down, everyone! We do something else.

FRAULEIN SCHNEIDER Something else? What else?

SCHULTZ What else? What? (*Suddenly inspired*) I will entertain!

FRAULEIN SCHNEIDER (*To the guests, apologetically*)   He has
had too much schnapps . . .

SCHULTZ   But I insist! So you will not think my only talent is
fruit. (HERR SCHULTZ *sees to it that everyone is seated and
ready*) Now—the only word you have to know in order to
understand my little song is the Yiddish word: *"meeskite."*
"Meeskite" means ugly, funny-looking. *"Meeskite"* means
. . . (*He sings*)
   Meeskite, Meeskite,
   Once upon a time there was a meeskite, meeskite,
   Looking in the mirror he would say, "What an
      awful shock,
   I got a face that could stop a clock."

   Meeskite, meeskite,
   Such a pity on him, he's a meeskite, meeskite,
   God up in his heaven left him out on a shaky limb,
   He put a meeskite on him.

But listen, he grew up. Even meeskites grow up. (*He sings
again*)

   And soon in the Chader (that means Hebrew school)
   He sat beside this little girl
   And when he asked her her name she replied,
   "I'm Pearl."
   He ran to the Zayda (that means grandfather)
   And said in that screechy voice of his,
   "You told me I was the homeliest!
   Well, Gramps, you're wrong. Pearl is!

   "Meeskite, meeskite,
   No one ever saw a bigger meeskite, meeskite,

Everywhere a flaw and maybe that is the reason why
I'm going to love her until I die.

"Meeskite, meeskite,
Oh, is it a pleasure she's a meeskite, meeskite,
She's the one I'll treasure, for I thought there could
    never be
A bigger meeskite than me."

So, they were married,
And in a year she turned and smiled:
"I'm afraid I am going to have . . . a child."
Nine months she carried,
Worrying how that child would look,
And all the cousins were worried too.
But what a turn fate took!

Gorgeous, gorgeous,
They produced a baby that was gorgeous, gorgeous,
Crowding round the cradle all the relatives aahed
    and oohed,
"He ought to pose for a baby food.

"Gorgeous, gorgeous,
Would I tell a lie? He's simply gorgeous, gorgeous,
Who'd have ever thought that we would see such a
    flawless gem
Out of two meeskites like them?"

Sing with me, somebody? Fraulein Schneider? Herr Ludwig
—we make a duet? Sally?
    (SALLY *comes forward and sings with* HERR SCHULTZ)

SCHULTZ and SALLY
>Meeskite, meeskite,
>Once upon a time there was a meeskite, meeskite,
>Looking in the mirror he would say, "What an
>>awful shock,
>I got a face that could stop a clock."

>Meeskite, meeskite,
>What's the good denying I'm a meeskite, meeskite,
>God up in his heaven made a joke for the world to see . . .
>>(SALLY *kisses* SCHULTZ *and sits*)

SCHULTZ
>He made a meeskite of me.

Now, wait! The story has a moral! All my stories have morals!

>Moral, moral,
>Yes indeed, the story has a moral, moral,
>Though you're not a beauty it is nevertheless
>>quite true,
>There may be beautiful things in you.

>Meeskite, meeskite,
>Listen to the fable of the meeskite, meeskite,
>Anyone responsible for loveliness, large or small,
>Is not a meeskite
>At all!

>(*All applaud except* ERNST, *who puts on his coat*)

ERNST Fraulein Schneider—Clifford—I wish to say good evening.

FRAULEIN SCHNEIDER But why so early?

ERNST I find that I do not belong here. I cannot stay.

FRAULEIN SCHNEIDER As you wish.

ERNST Fraulein—you and I are old acquaintances. I have sent you many new lodgers . . . So let me urge you—think what you are doing. This marriage is not advisable. I cannot put it too strongly. For your own welfare.

CLIFF What about Herr Schultz's welfare?

ERNST He is not a German.

FRAULEIN SCHNEIDER But he was born here!

ERNST He is not a German. Good evening.
(ERNST *goes to the door. As he reaches it,* FRAULEIN KOST *runs up to him*)

FRAULEIN KOST Herr Ludwig—wait! You are not leaving so early?

ERNST I do not find the party amusing.

FRAULEIN KOST Oh—but it is just beginning! Come—we will make it amusing—you and I, ja? (*She pulls* ERNST *back into the center of the shop*) Ladies and gentlemen— quiet please! Quiet! (*To* ERNST) Herr Ludwig—this is for you. (*She sings*)
> The sun on the meadow is summery warm,
> The stag in the forest runs free.
> But gather together to greet the storm,
> Tomorrow belongs to me.

Ja?
> The branch of the linden is leafy and green,
> The Rhine gives its gold to the sea.
> But somewhere a glory awaits unseen,
> Tomorrow belongs to me.

Herr Ludwig! Sing with me!
> (ERNST, *wearing the coat with the swastika armband, goes to her side. The guests form a circle around them, as if magnetically attracted*)

FRAULEIN KOST and ERNST (*singing*)
> The babe in his cradle is closing his eyes,
> The blossom embraces the bee.
> But soon, says a whisper, arise, arise,
> Tomorrow belong to me.

FRAULEIN KOST And now—everyone!
> (*The guests join in the singing—their voices growing louder and louder, even rather frightening. Only* FRAU-LEIN SCHNEIDER, HERR SCHULTZ, CLIFF *and* SALLY *remain outside the circle*)

FRAULEIN KOST, ERNST and GUESTS (*singing*)
Oh, Fatherland, Fatherland, show us the sign
Your children have waited to see.
The morning will come when the world is mine,
Tomorrow belongs to me.

(*As the song ends amid cheers and applause, the*
EMCEE *appears at the top of the spiral stairs—puffing
on a cigar. He takes in the scene:* FRAULEIN SCHNEIDER
and CLIFF *watching the singers with great concern—*
HERR SCHULTZ *and* SALLY *laughing, unaware of what
is happening. As the* EMCEE *descends the stairs the
fruit shop vanishes. The people on stage freeze against
a black background. The* EMCEE *slowly crosses the
stage—looking at everyone. Then he turns to the audience. He shrugs, he smiles, and exits*)

Blackout

Act Two

Eight girls dance out on stage—obviously the Kit Kat Klub chorus. They do a spirited dance of high kicks. Suddenly we are aware that one of the girls is the EMCEE. *As the dance begins to fall apart, we hear the ominous sound of military drums; the music changes to a martial version of "Tomorrow Belongs to Me" as the* EMCEE *and* GIRLS *goose-step offstage.*

Blackout

Inside HERR SCHULTZ's *shop,* HERR SCHULTZ *is taking down some of the remaining party decorations. Passers-by can be seen through the windows.* FRAULEIN SCHNEIDER *enters. She is obviously troubled.*

SCHULTZ   Fraulein Schneider—good morning!

FRAULEIN SCHNEIDER   Good morning, Herr Schultz.

SCHULTZ   New apples. Fresh off the tree. Perfection! (*He wipes one off and hands it to her*) Please . . .

FRAULEIN SCHNEIDER (*Refusing it*)   Perhaps later.

SCHULTZ   Such a party last evening! I have never been to a finer party! Such food! Such music! (*Suddenly very contrite*) Can you ever forgive me?

FRAULEIN SCHNEIDER   For what? A few glasses of schnapps?

SCHULTZ   I promise you—on our wedding day—no drinking —you will be proud of me.

FRAULEIN SCHNEIDER   I am already proud of you. But—as concerns the wedding . . .

SCHULTZ Yes?

FRAULEIN SCHNEIDER There are problems. New problems.

SCHULTZ If it is my drunkenness—I swear to you, Fraulein,
I am not an alcoholic.

FRAULEIN SCHNEIDER There is a thing—far more serious.

SCHULTZ A *new* problem . . . ?

FRAULEIN SCHNEIDER New to *me*—because I have not
thought about it. But at the party my eyes were opened.

SCHULTZ And?

FRAULEIN SCHNEIDER I saw that one can no longer dismiss
the Nazis. Because suddenly they are my friends and neighbors. And how many others? And—if so—is it possible they
will come to power?

SCHULTZ And you will be married to a Jew.

FRAULEIN SCHNEIDER (*Frightened*) I need my license to
rent my rooms! If they take it away . . .

SCHULTZ They will take nothing away. I promise you.
(*Softly*) I feel such tenderness for you. It is difficult to
express. Are we too old for words like "love"?

FRAULEIN SCHNEIDER Far too old. I am no Juliet. You are no
Romeo. We must be sensible.

SCHULTZ And live alone. How many meals have you eaten alone? A thousand? Ten thousand?

FRAULEIN SCHNEIDER Fifty thousand.

SCHULTZ Then *be* sensible. Governments come. Governments go. How much longer can we wait? (FRAULEIN SCHNEIDER *says nothing*) Let me peel you an orange . . .
(HERR SCHULTZ *takes a knife and starts peeling an orange rather clumsily. The underscoring of the music to "Married" is heard.* FRAULEIN SCHNEIDER *reaches for the orange*)

FRAULEIN SCHNEIDER *I will do it.*
(*She peels the orange. For a moment, we are back to the mood of their scenes in the first act*)

SCHULTZ (*singing*)
And the old despair
That was often there
Suddenly ceases to be.

For you wake one day,
Look around and say,
Somebody wonderful
Married me.
(*A brick crashes through the window.* FRAULEIN SCHNEIDER *and* HERR SCHULTZ *jump up*)

FRAULEIN SCHNEIDER You see? You see!

SCHULTZ It is nothing! Children on their way to school! Mischievous children! Nothing more! I assure you! (HERR SCHULTZ *runs out. We see him outside the broken window, looking for the culprit and questioning the onlookers. No one seems to have seen anything.* HERR SCHULTZ *comes back in*) Schoolchildren. Young—full of mischief. You understand?

FRAULEIN SCHNEIDER (*Slowly—thoughtfully*) I understand.

Lights fade

The EMCEE *enters, walking hand-in-hand with a gorilla.*
The gorilla is really rather attractive—as gorillas go. She
wears a chic little skirt and carries a handbag.

EMCEE (*singing*)
 I know what you're thinking—
 You wonder why I chose her
 Out of all the ladies in the world.
 That's just a first impression—
 What good's a first impression?
 If you knew her like I do,
 It would change your point of view.

 If you could see her through my eyes,
 You wouldn't wonder at all.
 If you could see her through my eyes,
 I guarantee you would fall like I did.

 When we're in public together,
 I hear society groan.
 But if they could see her through my eyes,
 Maybe they'd leave us alone.

 How can I speak of her virtues?
 I don't know where to begin:
 She's clever, she's smart, she reads music,
 She doesn't smoke or drink gin like I do.

Yet when we're walking together,
They sneer if I'm holding her hand.
But if they could see her through my eyes,
Maybe they'd all understand.
    (*They waltz*)
I understand your objection,
I grant you the problem's not small.
But if you could see her through my eyes,
She isn't a meeskite at all!
Alternate: She wouldn't look Jewish at all!

Blackout

CLIFF's *room.* SALLY *is dressing to go out.* CLIFF *enters, wearing a coat.*

SALLY Cliff! I've been waiting so anxiously! Did you get a job?

CLIFF I'll try again tomorrow.
(*They kiss*)

SALLY And you'll find something! I'm sure of it! President of a bank!

CLIFF They're closed.

SALLY Guess who visited me today! Bobby and Victor! From the Kit Kat! You remember them?

CLIFF How could I forget them?

SALLY They say business at the Klub's way off since I left. And Lulu—one of the girls—had her teeth knocked out by a Lithuanian. Oh—and Max . . . you remember Max? He's fallen madly in love. And it turns out she's a dedicated Communist *and* a dedicated virgin. Isn't that heaven!

CLIFF Heaven.

SALLY   Would you simply *hate* it if I went back to work at the Klub?

CLIFF   I sure would.

SALLY   But we need the money so badly!

CLIFF   Not *that* badly.

SALLY   I don't understand you. Really I don't. First you tell me you're not going to Paris for Ernst any more—even though it does seem the very easiest way in the world to make money . . .

CLIFF   Or the hardest. (SALLY *looks at him blankly*) Someday I've simply got to sit you down and read you a newspaper. You'll be amazed at what's going on.

SALLY   You mean—politics? But what has *that* to do with us?

CLIFF   You're right. *Nothing* has anything to do with us. Sally, can't you see—if you're not against all this, you're for it—or you might as well be.

SALLY   At any rate, the Kit Kat Klub is the most *un*political place in Berlin. Even *you*'ve got to admit *that*.

CLIFF   Sally—do me a favor? Let *me* earn the money for this family. At least give me the chance. If I can't even get something—washing beer glasses—then we'll talk about you working in some cabaret. And after you've tried every other club in Berlin, we might even talk about the Kit Kat Klub. And I imagine I'll still say no. But—who knows? By that time I may be almost ready to listen to reason. Okay? *(There is a knock at the door)* Come in!

> *(The door opens.* FRAULEIN SCHNEIDER *is there. She carries a large gift-wrapped package)*

FRAULEIN SCHNEIDER   I intrude?

SALLY   No. No. Come in, Fraulein Schneider.

CLIFF *(To* FRAULEIN SCHNEIDER*)*   Have you seen Herr Schultz this morning? *(*FRAULEIN SCHNEIDER *nods)* How is he? A little hung-over?
> *(She nods again)*

SALLY   Fraulein Schneider—is that the fruit bowl? Is something wrong with it?
> *(*SALLY *indicates the package* FRAULEIN SCHNEIDER *is carrying)*

FRAULEIN SCHNEIDER *(Shaking her head)*   I cannot keep it.

SALLY   But why?

FRAULEIN SCHNEIDER   An engagement present. But there is no engagement.

SALLY   What do you mean?

96

FRAULEIN SCHNEIDER   We have—reconsidered—Herr Schultz and I.

CLIFF   Fraulein, you can't give up that way!

FRAULEIN SCHNEIDER   Oh, yes! I can. That is easy to say! Easy for you. Fight! And—if you fail—what does it matter? You pack your belongings. You move to Paris. And if you do not like Paris—where? It is easy for *you*. But if you were *me* . . .
     (*She sings*)
     With time rushing by,
     What would you do?

     With the clock running down,
     What would you do?
     The young always have the cure—
     Being brave, being sure
     And free,
     But imagine if you were me.

     Alone like me,
     And this is the only world you know.
     Some rooms to let—
     The sum of a lifetime, even so.

     I'll take your advice.
     What would you do?

     Would you pay the price?
     What would you do?

Suppose simply keeping still
Means you manage until the end?
What would you do,
My brave young friend?

Grown old like me,
With neither the will nor wish to run;
Grown tired like me,
Who hurries for bed when day is done;
Grown wise like me,
Who isn't at war with anyone—
Not anyone!
With a storm in the wind,
What would you do?

Suppose you're one frightened voice
Being told what the choice must be.

Go on, tell me,
I will listen.

What would you do
If you were me?

CLIFF   Aren't you forgetting something? If you marry Herr
Schultz—whatever problems come up—you'll still have
each other.

FRAULEIN SCHNEIDER   All my life I have managed for myself
—and it is too old a habit to change. I have battled alone,
and I have survived. There was a war—and I survived.
There was a revolution—and I survived. There was an infla-

tion—billions of marks for one loaf of bread—but I survived! And if the Nazis come—I will survive. And if the Communists come—I will still be here—renting these rooms! For, in the end, what other choice have I? This—is my world! (*Softly*) I regret—very much—returning the fruit bowl. It is truly magnificent. I regret—everything.

(FRAULEIN SCHNEIDER *exits*)

SALLY   Oh, Cliff—how terrible. Should I speak to her?

CLIFF   What could you say?

SALLY   Oh—that it will all work itself out.

CLIFF   I don't think she'd believe you.

SALLY   It seems *nobody* believes me today. It's quite obvious *you* don't—about Max. If he wants me back at the Klub, it's not for the reason you think. Did it ever occur to you I just might be a tremendous asset to that Klub? The fact is, they're waiting there this very minute—to rehearse *my* numbers. So I really must go.

(CLIFF *has gone to his typewriter, opened it, and started to dust it with his handkerchief*)

CLIFF   The fact is, you're going a lot farther than the Kit Kat Klub.

SALLY   I *am*?

CLIFF   Home. (SALLY *looks at him blankly*) America—since you won't go to England.

SALLY   You're joking!
(CLIFF *indicates the typewriter*)

CLIFF   I'm going to sell this. The money should get us as far as Paris. And I'll cable home for steamship fare.

SALLY   What are you talking about?

CLIFF   Leaving Berlin—as soon as possible. Tomorrow!

SALLY   But we love it here!

CLIFF   Sally—wake up! The party in Berlin is *over!* It was lots of fun, but it's over. And what is Berlin doing *now?* Vomiting in the street.

SALLY   How ugly, Cliff!

CLIFF   You're damn right it's ugly! And it's going to get a lot worse. So how could we live here? How could we raise a family?

SALLY   But is America the answer? Running away to America?

CLIFF   We're *not* running away. There's no place to run to. We are going home.

SALLY   Oh, certainly—that's fine for *you.* But what about *me?* My career?

CLIFF   You've got a new career.

SALLY   But I can work at the Klub for several months at least. And then—in November—oh, Cliff, I want the world for our baby—all the most elegant, expensive things.

CLIFF   We'll talk about it tomorrow—on the train.
(CLIFF *finishes preening the typewriter. He closes it and starts for the door with it*)

SALLY   Cliff—wait! We can't just—uproot our lives—that quickly!

CLIFF   Oh, no? You give me one hour! And don't move! (*He pushes her into a chair*) Sit down! Or— better yet— start packing! (*He puts a suitcase on the bed*) There's plenty to do! (CLIFF *goes toward the door. Then he reaches into a pocket, takes out a coin and gives it to* SALLY *in a gesture of reconciliation*) Here. *Call* the Klub. Tell them goodbye.
(CLIFF *exits.* SALLY *looks at the coin. Then she makes up her mind. She springs up, grabs her fur coat and rushes out the door.*)

Blackout

A crowded evening at the Kit Kat Klub. CLIFF *enters.*

WAITER   Good evening, sir.
(CLIFF *sees* SALLY *at the bar and goes to her*)

CLIFF   What the hell are you doing here? I—

SALLY   May I speak for a moment?

CLIFF   Get your coat! I'm taking you home!

SALLY (*Pulling* CLIFF *to a table*) Please, Cliff! If we go to America, there's no assurance you can get a job. There *is* a great deal of unemployment there. You've said so yourself.

CLIFF   I'll find *something*.

SALLY   Maybe, but *this* is sure!

CLIFF   This! What the hell is *this*? You keep talking about *this* as if it really existed. When are you going to realize, the only way you got this job is by sleeping with somebody!

SALLY   That's not true!

CLIFF   And the only way you'll get a job in New York or Paris or London is by sleeping with someone else! But you're sleeping with *me* these days!

SALLY   Shut up, Cliff!

CLIFF   Sally, face it. Say goodbye to Berlin, Max, this dump, everybody. Believe me, they'll never even know you've left.

SALLY   I've got to change for my next number.
   (*She runs off*)

CLIFF   Sally!
   (*But she is gone.* CLIFF *is trembling with anger. The phone on his table lights up. He answers it*)

CLIFF   Hello.
   (*A spot picks up* ERNST LUDWIG, *who is sitting at a table with an attractive girl*)

ERNST   (*Into his phone*)   Clifford—this is Ernst Ludwig. I am at table nine. Will you join me for a drink?

CLIFF   Not now, Ernst.

ERNST   I have been trying to reach you at Fraulein Schneider's—but you do not answer. I have another urgent errand for you.

CLIFF   Sorry.

ERNST   This time I pay—one hundred and fifty marks.

CLIFF   The answer is no.

ERNST   But what is wrong, Clifford? You are angry with me?

CLIFF   I am?

ERNST   It is because of the party last evening? If you were a German, you would understand these things.

CLIFF   Goodbye, Ernst.
        (CLIFF *hangs up.* ERNST *stands and comes toward* CLIFF, *who is anxious to follow* SALLY)

ERNST   Wait! It is very important—this errand. I pay—two hundred marks.

CLIFF   Go to hell.
        (CLIFF *tries to leave.* ERNST *grabs him*)

ERNST   But what is wrong with you? I don't understand!

CLIFF   Take your hands off me—
        (ERNST *does*)

ERNST   Clifford—I know you need the money. So why won't you go? It is because of that Jew at the party?
        (CLIFF *socks* ERNST, *knocking him down. Immediately two men wearing Nazi armbands jump on* CLIFF—

*beating him unconscious. They drag him out of the
Klub as the patrons watch.* ERNST *rises and goes back
to his table. The* EMCEE *appears—laughing rather
hysterically—as if the fight were part of the floor show)*

EMCEE And now—once again—Fraulein Sally Bowles!
(SALLY *enters and sings)*

SALLY

What good is sitting alone in your room?
Come hear the music play.
Life is a cabaret, old chum,
Come to the cabaret.

Put down the knitting, the book and the broom,
Time for a holiday.
Life is a cabaret, old chum,
Come to the cabaret.

Come taste the wine,
Come hear the band,
Come blow a horn, start celebrating.
Right this way, your table's waiting.

No use permitting some prophet of doom
To wipe every smile away.
Life is a cabaret, old chum,
Come to the cabaret.

I used to have a girl friend known as Elsie
With whom I shared four sordid rooms in Chelsea.
She wasn't what you'd call a blushing flower;
As a matter of fact, she rented by the hour.

The day she died the neighbors came to snicker,
"Well, that's what comes of too much pills and liquor."
But when I saw her laid out like a queen,
She was the happiest corpse I'd ever seen.

I think of Elsie to this very day.
I remember how she'd turn to me and say . . .
    (SALLY *has walked off the Kit Kat Klub stage. She
    heads directly downstage as the Kit Kat Klub dis-
    appears.* SALLY *stands alone*)
What good is sitting alone in your room?
Come hear the music play.
Life is a cabaret, old chum,
Come to the cabaret.

Put down the knitting, the book and the broom,
Time for a holiday.
Life is a cabaret, old chum,
Come to the cabaret.

And as for me, as for me,
I made my mind up back in Chelsea.
When I go, I'm going like Elsie!

Start by admitting from cradle to tomb
Isn't that long a stay.
Life is a cabaret, old chum,
Only a cabaret, old chum,
And I love a cabaret!

Blackout

CLIFF's *room. It is late morning.* CLIFF *is busily packing. His face is bandaged and he moves a little stiffly.*

There is a knock at the door. CLIFF *rushes to the door and opens it.* HERR SCHULTZ *is there.*

CLIFF (*Disappointed*) Good morning, Herr Schultz.
(HERR SCHULTZ *enters. He has a suitcase in one hand and a brown paper bag in the other*)

SCHULTZ Excuse me—but I have come to say goodbye.
(*He sees* CLIFF's *bandages*)

CLIFF It's nothing. A little accident. Where are you going?

SCHULTZ I have taken a room on the other side of the Nollendorfplatz. I think it will be easier for *her.* (*He notes all the packing*) You are leaving also? You and Fraulein Bowles?

CLIFF We're going home. To America.

SCHULTZ America! I have sometimes thought of going there—

CLIFF Why don't you? The way things look here—

SCHULTZ But it will pass—I promise you!

CLIFF   I hope you're right.

SCHULTZ   I *know* I am right! Because I understand the Germans . . . After all, what am *I*? A German. (*The door opens and* SALLY *enters. She looks ill and exhausted. She wears a rather thin dress and is carrying her purse. She stands at the door.* HERR SCHULTZ *goes to her*) Ah—Fraulein Sally! I have come to say goodbye . . . all good fortune.

SALLY   Herr Schultz.

SCHULTZ   I have brought a small farewell gift. (*He gives* SALLY *the paper bag*) Seville oranges. Delicious.
(SALLY *hugs him. Then* CLIFF *and* HERR SCHULTZ *shake hands*)

CLIFF   Goodbye, Herr Schultz. And I wish you *mazel*.
(*He exits*)

SCHULTZ   *Mazel.* That is what we all need.

CLIFF   (*Artificially cheerful*) I've finished your packing. You've got a lot of stuff, lady. You won't be able to find a thing. (SALLY *says nothing*) We're going to Paris today . . . remember?

SALLY   (*Looking at him*)   Going . . . with *that* face?
(*Her voice sounds very, very weary*)

CLIFF   I was in a little fight last night. Did you hear about it? (SALLY *nods*) You should see the other two guys. (*Pause*)

Not a mark *on* them. (*He looks at his watch*) Do you realize how late it is? Almost time to go to the station . . .

SALLY   The fact *is,* Cliff—

CLIFF   Don't say it. Whatever it is. Let's just—forget the last twelve hours. Forget what I said at the Kit Kat Klub. Forget you've gotten even with me staying out all night . . . okay? (*He takes her hand*) You're so cold. Where's your coat? Your fur coat?

SALLY   You know what I'd love? A spot of gin! We've got some, don't we? I mean—I think one *must!*

CLIFF   First thing in the morning? How about a Prairie Oyster?

SALLY   Gin!
(*She gets herself a drink*)

CLIFF   That can't be good for expectant mothers. We'll have to get some books on the subject. You know, I suddenly realize I don't know a damn thing about pregnancy. Where's your coat? Did you leave it at the Klub, or was it stolen?

SALLY   I left it at the doctor's office.

CLIFF   Were you sick last night? Is that why you didn't come home?

SALLY   Hals and beinbruch. It means neck and leg break. It's supposed to stop it from happening—though I doubt it does.

I doubt you can stop *anything* happening. Any more than you can change people. I mean . . .

CLIFF   *What* do you mean?

SALLY   I mean—I'm not perfect. Far from it! I meet someone and I make all sorts of enormous promises. And then there's an argument—or something else ugly—and I suddenly realize I can't keep those promises—not possibly! Because I am still *me!*

CLIFF   Sally, what are you talking about?

SALLY   Oh, darling—you're such an innocent. Really! My one regret is I honestly believe you'd have been a wonderful father. And I'm sure someday you *will* be. Oh yes, and I've another regret: That greedy doctor! I'm going to miss my fur coat. (CLIFF *slaps her*) I'm glad you did that. Isn't it funny it always ends this way? Even when I finally *do* love someone terribly—for the first time. But it's still not —quite—enough. I'd spoil it, Cliff. I'd run away with the first exciting thing that came along. I guess I really am a rather strange and extraordinary person. (CLIFF *is packing his bag*) Cliff . . . I'm sorry. I'm so dreadfully, dreadfully sorry. Because . . . the truth is . . . I really would have liked . . .
> (*She can't go on.* CLIFF *finishes his preparations for leaving. Then he takes out his wallet. He removes one of the railroad tickets and puts it down on the table*)

CLIFF   This is your ticket to Paris. You can cash it in . . . or tear it up . . . or do whatever you want with it. (CLIFF *takes his suitcase and goes to the door*) Sally . . . if . . . for any reason . . . you need to get in touch with me . . . in Paris . . . the American Express office. (SALLY *looks at him*) I'll be there at least a week.

(CLIFF *obviously can't force himself to go out the door.* SALLY *wipes her eyes. She lights a cigarette in the long, long holder. She smiles—making a tremendous effort to be the old* SALLY *again for a moment*)

SALLY But—the truth is—Cliff: I've always rather *hated* Paris.

(*She puffs on her cigarette. She smiles at* CLIFF, *as if telling him that she will be perfectly fine without him*)

CLIFF (*Sadly*) Oh, Sally. Goodbye.

SALLY Goodbye, Cliff. Dedicate your book to me!

(CLIFF *exits, closing the door behind him.* SALLY *takes the long cigarette holder out of her mouth. Her smile fades. She turns to the door as the lights dim very slowly*)

SCENE 7

Before the lights come up we hear

LOUDSPEAKER VOICE Letzte ansage! Berlin-Paris Express abfahrt vier uhr bahnsteig siebzehn. Alle einsteigen, bitte! *Letzte ansage!*
> (*The lights go up on a railroad compartment.* CLIFF *is alone in it. He has a writing pad on his lap, a pencil in his hand. Two* CUSTOMS OFFICERS *enter from the corridor*)

OFFICER Deutsche grenzkontrolle. Ihren pass, bitte. (CLIFF *hands it to him. He hands it back to* CLIFF) I hope you have enjoyed your stay in Germany, Mr. Bradshaw. And you will return soon again?

CLIFF It's not very likely.

OFFICER You did not find our country beautiful?

CLIFF (*Tonelessly*) Yes, I found it—beautiful.

OFFICER A good journey, sir.
> (*The* OFFICER *tips his cap and exits.* CLIFF *looks at his writing pad. He crosses out a few words, then adds a few. He reads what he has written*)

CLIFF "There was a cabaret and there was a master of cere-monies and there was a city called Berlin in a country called

Germany—and it was the end of the world and I was danc-
ing with Sally Bowles—and we were both fast asleep . . ."
(*Singing*)
Willkommen, bienvenue, welcome,
Fremde, étranger, stranger.
(*The* EMCEE *has entered and come downstage. He
moves his lips soundlessly as* CLIFF *sings. Then he be-
gins singing along with* CLIFF)

CLIFF and EMCEE
Glücklich zu sehen,
Je suis enchanté,
Happy to see you.
(*Then* CLIFF *stops singing and the* EMCEE *finishes
alone as the train moves up stage*)

EMCEE
Bleibe, reste, stay,
Willkommen, bienvenue, welcome,
Im cabaret, au cabaret, to cabaret!

Meine Damen und Herren—Mesdames et Messieurs—
Ladies and Gentlemen. Where are your troubles now? For-
gotten? I told you so! We have no troubles here. Here
life is beautiful—the girls are beautiful—even the orchestra
is beautiful.
(*The* GIRL ORCHESTRA *appears onstage as do the char-
acters from the opening scene, but this time the picture
and the mood are much different. The girls are not as
pretty, German uniforms and swastika armbands are
apparent; it is not as bright, a dream-like quality pre-
vails. Dissonant strains of "Willkommen" are heard.*

Then from among the moving people, we see HERR
SCHULTZ)

SCHULTZ   Just children. Mischievous children on their way to
school. You understand.
(*The people move again and we see* FRAULEIN
SCHNEIDER)

FRAULEIN SCHNEIDER   I understand. One does what one
must.
(*Again the people move and we see* SALLY)

SALLY   It'll all work out. It's only politics, and what's that
got to do with us?

FRAULEIN SCHNEIDER   I must be sensible. If the Nazis come
—what other choice have I?

SCHULTZ   I know I am right—because I understand the Germans. After all, what am I? A German.
(*Suddenly* SALLY *is lifted high on a chair*)

SALLY (*singing*)
I made my mind up back in Chelsea.
When I go I'm going like Elsie.
(SALLY *is lowered. The people gradually fade away*)
. . . from cradle to tomb
Isn't that long a stay.
Life is a cabaret, old chum,
Life is a cabaret, old chum,
Life is a cabaret.

(SALLY *disappears into the darkness—leaving the* EMCEE *alone on the stage.*)

EMCEE

Auf wiedersehen!

À bientôt!

(*The* EMCEE *bows, then suddenly vanishes. The stage is empty except for the street lamps, the mirror, and then, glowing in the darkness, the "Cabaret" sign.*)